NATIVE AMERICAN LITERATURE

THE JUNIOR LIBRARY OF
AMERICAN INDIANS

NATIVE AMERICAN LITERATURE

Katherine Gleason

CHELSEA JUNIORS

a division of CHELSEA HOUSE PUBLISHERS

FRONTISPIECE: Herman Morton Stoops' illustration for Luther Standing Bear's *Stories of the Sioux* (1934). The illustration was based on sketches by Oglala Sioux Yellow Bird.

CHAPTER TITLE ORNAMENT: An Arapaho symbol meaning "person."

English-language words italicized in the text can be found in the glossary at the back of the book.

Chelsea House Publishers
EDITORIAL DIRECTOR Richard Rennert
ART DIRECTOR Sara Davis
PRODUCTION MANAGER Pamela Loos
PICTURE EDITOR Judy Hasday

The Junior Library of American Indians
SENIOR EDITOR Martin Schwabacher

Staff for NATIVE AMERICAN LITERATURE
ASSOCIATE EDITOR Therese De Angelis
EDITORIAL ASSISTANT Kristine Brennan
DESIGNER Steve Schildbach
PICTURE RESEARCHER Sandy Jones
COVER ILLUSTRATOR Hal Just

3 5 7 9 8 6 4 2

Library of Congress Cataloging-in-Publication Data

Gleason, Katherine.
Native American Literature / Katherine Gleason
  p. cm.—(The Junior Library of American Indians)
Includes index.
Summary: Introduces Native American authors and provides a glimpse into their culture, historical perspective, and world-view.
ISBN   0-7910-2477-6 (hc.)
              0-7910-2478-4 (pbk.)
1. American Literature—Indian authors—History and criticism—Juvenile Literature. 2. Authors, American—Biography—Juvenile literature. 3. Authors, Indian—Biography—Juvenile literature. 4. Indians in literature—Juvenile literature.
[American Literature—Indian Authors. 2. Authors, American. 3. Authors, Indian. 4. Indians in literature.] I. Title. II. Series.
PS153.I52G54   1996   95-40562
810.9'3520397—dc20   CIP
                                                    AC

CONTENTS

CHAPTER **1**

The First American Authors

In the beginning, Awonawilona lived alone in the universe. Nothing else existed, and space was filled with fog and steam. Then Awonawilona, who was both male and female, created the clouds and waters from its breath and later formed the rest of the universe.

This universe consists of nine layers. The earth, which occupies the middle level, is a large round island surrounded by oceans. Lakes, rivers, and springs on the earth are connected to the oceans by underground linkages. The sky is an upside-down bowl of stone, resting above the earth. Each of the other eight layers of the universe is home to different kinds of animals, birds, and trees.

At first, people lived under the earth's surface in the fourth layer of the universe, which is deep inside the body of Earth Mother. These people did not look like humans do today. Their bodies were covered with slime, they had webbed hands and feet, and they had tails. They did not realize how strange they looked because they could not see clearly in the darkness of the earth.

After a while, Sun Father decided to bring people out of the earth because he was lonely. Sun Father told his twin sons, the War Gods, to lead the people outside. The War Gods helped them climb up a ladder from inside the earth and then changed the people's appearance, removing the slime from their bodies and giving them normal hands and feet.

This story of the creation of the earth is one of the oldest stories in America. The Zuni Indians told this tale long before the first English word was ever spoken in America. When European explorers first came to North America, there were about 18 million people already living on the continent. These people came to be called American Indians or Native Americans. Five million Native Americans lived in the area that is now the United States. They belonged to many different tribes who spoke almost 200 languages. About 150 of these languages are still spoken today.

All of these Native American peoples had a wealth of stories, myths, and fables. But for many years, most Americans were taught that American literature was born with the arrival of English colonists in the 1600s. Most non-Indians had little understanding of the rich *cultures* and long histories of the millions of Native Americans who lived in what is now the United States.

The true history of literature in America, however, goes back thousands of years. It begins with the *oral traditions* of the Native Americans. Oral traditions are stories, songs, and ceremonies that were passed on from generation to generation. The Indian tribes that lived north of Mexico did not have a system of writing, so stories and songs had to be remembered and handed down from parents to children. Oral traditions were used to impart *values* such as cooperation, generosity, helpfulness, and respect for older, more experienced people.

As white people spread across the land, the traditional lifestyles of the Native Americans were disrupted. Tribes were forced from their land, and many people died from disease and warfare. Tragically,

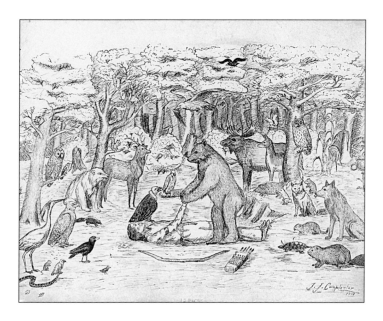

Raising the Slain Hero *by Jesse Complanter, who recorded stories of the Seneca Indians in* Legends of the Longhouse.

some tribes were destroyed, and their knowledge has been lost. Those tribes that survived the invasion of the whites underwent drastic changes as the U.S. government tried to make them give up their languages, religious beliefs, and customs.

With these changes, the Native American oral traditions were in danger of disappearing. However, as Native Americans learned to speak and write in English, they began to record their tribes' histories, beliefs, and stories. Writing made it possible to preserve their traditions for future generations of Indians and to describe their rich cultures to non-Indians. Some Indian authors used the Latin alphabet (the alphabet used to write English) to write in their native language. In this way they preserved not only their oral traditions but their language itself.

One Native American invented a special system of writing for his tribe. Sequoyah, a Cherokee silversmith, developed a system with 86 symbols. Each symbol stood for one syllable in the Cherokee language. In 1821, the Cherokee tribal council approved his work. They used his invention to write the constitution of the Cherokee Nation, which was founded in 1827. The following year, a Cherokee-English newspaper called the *Cherokee Phoenix* appeared.

Most Native American authors, however, wrote in English. They used English for several reasons. Many wanted to communicate with non-Indians and with Indians who spoke languages other than their own. They also wanted their words to travel. In the days before the telephone, the written word could go places that the spoken word could not. Since many tribes did not have a way to write in their tribal languages, they used English instead.

For many Indians, English became their primary language. As the U.S. government forced the Indians off their land and onto *reservations*, Native American children throughout the country were sent away from their families to government schools

Some Indian tribes used pictures to record stories and historical events. This buffalo hide is painted with figures from the stories of the Kiowa Indians. The human figure is Saynday, the supernatural creator of the world. Below him are two Zemoguani, great horned fish who were believed to live in underwater caves and sometimes seize unlucky swimmers.

so that they would forget their tribal ways. In these schools, the children were not allowed to speak their own languages. They were taught to speak, read, and write only in English.

Some Indians used their educations to help their people. As they witnessed the destruction of their civilizations, Native American writers made powerful appeals for justice in the whites' own language. They spread the word about the theft of their land and the abuse of their people, and they educated whites about the complex civilizations that were being destroyed.

Native American authors such as Sarah

Winnemucca wrote passionate pleas for the rights of their people. While many whites were eager to take over the Indians' land, Winnemucca forced them to face the human cost of these military conquests: "For shame! For shame! You dare to cry out Liberty, when you hold us in places against our will, driving us from place to place as if we were beasts."

As the number of Native American writers has increased, more and more variety has emerged in the style and subject matter of their work. They have created a wealth of poems, plays, and *novels* ranging from best-selling mysteries to award-winning stories for children. They have used their art both to educate and to entertain. In a rapidly changing world, Native American authors continue to write for and about the times they live in.

Native American authors have a rich tradition. They have kept the ancient stories alive. They have invented new stories and heroes. Their work from long ago and from the present day has helped to explain what it means to be an American. ▲

Mountain Chief, a Blackfoot Indian, interprets a tribal song as it is played on a phonograph by Frances Densmore in 1916. Densmore was one of the first recorders and translators of Native American music.

CHAPTER 2

The Oral Tradition

The oral traditions of Native Americans were central to their way of life. Indian children did not have schools. They learned everything they needed to know from their parents and other adults, often in the form of stories. Storytelling usually took place in the evening, after the day's work was finished. Many tribes spent the cold winter months gathered around the fire sharing their *myths* and tales. Each tribe had a wealth of stories that taught children about their history and religion and provided examples of the way members of the tribe were expected to behave. By listening to traditional stories, Native Americans learned about the world and their place in it.

Each tribe has a myth about the beginning of the world. The most common creation stories are known as earth-diver myths. They are told by many of the tribes that once lived in the Great Lakes area. According to these stories, land was created from mud that was brought up from the bottom of the sea by an animal (the earth-diver). The Iroquois creation story is one example of the earth-diver myth.

The Iroquois were a powerful group of tribes that once lived in New York State. They tell of a time before there were humans, when the Sky People lived in a world above our own. In the Sky World, all light came from the white blossoms of the great tree that stood before the lodge of the Sky Chief. One day, the troublesome Firedragon, who loved to spread rumors, told Sky Chief that his wife, Sky Woman, was in love with another man. In a fit of anger and jealousy, Sky Chief uprooted the great tree and pushed Sky Woman through the hole where it had stood.

Sky Woman fell toward the dark waters below, for at that time there was no land. The birds, feeling sorry for her, gently

This illustration from N. Scott Momaday's The Way to Rainy Mountain *depicts the Kiowa story about the formation of Devil's Tower in Wyoming.*

caught Sky Woman and carried her slowly downward. The sea animals hurried to make a place for her. Turtle said that he would support a world on his back. The other animals plunged to the bottom of the sea looking for some earth. Duck tried but could not reach the bottom. Loon and Beaver also tried, but without success. Finally, Muskrat dove to the bottom and returned with a mouthful of earth, which he placed on Turtle's back. This became the world. The light from the great tree shone through the hole in the sky and became the sun. By the time Sky Woman landed on Turtle's back, everything was ready for her, with plants and trees beginning to grow.

Other myths explain the creation of certain things in a tribe's territory. The Kiowa have a story that describes the formation of Devils Tower, a huge, eerie-looking rock formation with steep grooved walls that rises suddenly from the Wyoming grasslands.

One day long ago, a boy was playing with his seven sisters. He began to tremble, and before his sisters' eyes he turned into a ferocious grizzly bear. The terrified sisters hid behind a large tree stump. The tree stump spoke to the sisters, telling them to climb onto it. As the sisters climbed atop the stump it began to grow, rising straight toward the sky. The angry bear clawed the tree stump, forming grooves in the bark, but soon his sisters were out of reach. The stump continued to rise and hurled the sisters up into the sky, where they became the seven stars of the Big Dipper.

Many Native American myths tell of the adventures of superhuman beings who lived in ancient times. These stories teach lessons about the rewards of bravery and good behavior and the punishment received by wrongdoers. Other popular characters are the tricksters. Tricksters are usually self-centered and think only about fulfilling their own desires, regardless of the consequences. They often suffer for their selfish behavior. The Sioux, Kwakiutl, Pueblo, Apache, and other tribes tell stories about a trickster named Coyote.

The Blackfoot Indians of the Western Plains tell of a race between two tricksters, Old Man and Coyote. One day, Old Man saw some deer and elk playing a game of follow-the-leader. Old Man joined the game, sang a song, and, as the leader, led the animals to the edge of a cliff. Old Man jumped down and was knocked senseless. When he recovered, he called to the elk to follow his lead. The animals were afraid of being hurt, but Old Man said, "Oh, it's nice and soft here.

Jump now!" The elk jumped down and were killed by the fall. Then Old Man called to the deer to jump down. The deer said, "No, we shall not jump down because the elk are all killed," but Old Man insisted that the elk were only pretending. So the deer jumped down and were also killed. Old Man butchered the animals and carried the meat back to his camp.

Soon Coyote came by, wearing a shell around his neck. One of his legs was tied up as though it was badly hurt. Coyote asked Old Man for something to eat. Old Man offered to give Coyote meat in exchange for his shell, but Coyote refused because the shell was his protective medicine. Then Old Man noticed that Coyote's leg was bandaged and said, "Well, you may race me for a meal." Coyote answered, "I am hurt. I cannot run." But Old Man insisted that they run a race to a point far from his camp and back again, and Coyote finally agreed.

On the way out from the camp, Coyote ran very slowly, crying for Old Man to wait for him. But when the two reached the turning point, clever Coyote suddenly tore the bandage off his leg and sped back to the camp, leaving Old Man far behind. Coyote called to all the coyotes and mice and other animals, telling them to come to Old Man's camp for a good meal, and they feasted on Old Man's meat. Old Man ran and ran, trying to get back to his camp before all his food was gone, calling out pitifully all the while, "Leave me some meat, leave me some meat."

Aside from stories, another important part of the oral traditions are the *chants* used in ceremonies. Some tribes have special words or whole languages that are used only in ceremonies. The Sioux Indians use two special languages in their ceremonies— *wakan iye* and *hanbloblaka*. During ceremonies the participants recite many long prayers from memory.

The Night Chant of the Navajo Indians lasts for eight and a half days. This ceremony is used to cure a sick member of the tribe. Since many people participate in this ceremony, it also helps to bring the community together. On the last day of the Night Chant, all of the songs of the past eight days are repeated throughout the night. The ceremony ends at daybreak, when the healed person faces east to inhale the breath of dawn.

One of the best-known prayers from the Night Chant describes the Tsegihi, a shrine in the Canyon de Chelly in northeastern Arizona, the center of the Navajo homeland.

During the Navajo Indians'
Night Chant, a priest creates
a sand painting, forming
holy images from powdered
minerals. This sand painting
was used in a 1954 cere-
mony to heal a sick child.

The prayer calls the Tsegihi a house made
of dawn.

Tsegihi!
House made of dawn.
House made of evening light.
House made of the dark cloud.
House made of the dark mist.
House made of the female rain.
House made of pollen.
House made of grasshoppers.
Dark cloud is at the door.
The trail out of it is dark cloud.

The zigzag lightning stands high upon it.
Male deity!
Your offering I make.
I have prepared a smoke for you.
Restore my feet for me.
Restore my legs for me.
Restore my body for me.
Restore my mind for me.
Restore my voice for me.
This very day take out your spell for me.
Your spell remove for me.
You have taken it away for me.
Far off it has gone.
Happily I recover.
Happily my interior becomes cool.
Happily I go forth.
My interior feeling cool, I may walk.
No longer sore, I may walk.
Impervious to pain I may walk.
With lively feelings I may walk.
As it used to be long ago, I may walk.
Happily I may walk.
Happily with abundant dark clouds may I walk.
Happily with abundant showers may I walk.
Happily with abundant plants may I walk.
Happily on a trail of pollen may I walk.
Happily may I walk.
Being as it used to be long ago, may I walk.
May it be beautiful before me.
May it be beautiful behind me.
May it be beautiful below me.
May it be beautiful all around me.
In beauty it is finished.
In beauty it is finished.

The repetition of words helps to give this prayer its rhythm and beauty and to create the feeling of a gradual transformation from

An Ojibwa chief stands outside the lodge of the Midéwiwin, a society of medicine men and women. Members of the Midéwiwin learn hundreds of songs, which preserve the ancient teachings and beliefs of the society.

sickness to peace and well-being.

Songs make up the largest part of Native American oral tradition. In some tribes, songs are central to all aspects of life. The Ojibwa regard singing as one of the greatest pleasures. The Pima believe that many of their songs were made by the creator at the beginning of the world. Among the Plains Indians, young men have visions during which they learn dream songs from spirits. The Papago Indians of the Southwest see songs as a form of magic. Planters from the Papago tribe sing a special song to their corn at night to help it grow. When the Papago sing this song, they say that they are "singing up the corn."

Native Americans have traditionally placed great value on public speaking. In tribal councils, everyone listened attentively as people took turns voicing their opinions. Those who spoke *eloquently* earned respect and often were chosen to be leaders. One leader who is remembered for his moving speeches is Tecumseh. A member of the Shawnee tribe, Tecumseh tried to

Native Americans and British commanders hold a council in 1763 following Pontiac's War. Even enemies were often impressed by Native Americans' powerful speeches.

unite Indians of all tribes in defending their land against the whites who were rapidly moving westward. Tecumseh's intelligence and his convincing speeches won many supporters. In this speech from 1811, Tecumseh explains why the Indians must continue their fight against the whites:

> Where today are the Pequot? Where are the Narragansett, the Mohican, the Pocanet, and other powerful tribes of our people? They have vanished before the avarice and oppression of the white man, as snow before the summer sun. . . . Will we let ourselves be destroyed in our turn, without making an effort worthy of our race? Shall we, without a struggle, give up our homes, our lands, bequeathed to us by the Great Spirit? The graves of our dead and everything that is dear and sacred to us? . . . I know you will say with me, Never! Never!

The oral tradition is still important to Native Americans. People from many tribes tell the old stories and create new versions. Some ancient stories have been kept alive in the books that Indian authors have written. These stories continue to teach Indian children about their tribes' rich histories. And they help non-Indians to understand the many peoples who once populated North America. ◮

Sarah Winnemucca's Life Among the Piutes *made white readers aware of the terrible suffering that the U.S. government brought upon her tribe.*

CHAPTER 3

Early Writers

Five hundred years ago, when Europeans first arrived in what is now the United States, Native Americans had their first contact with a written language. Native Americans first learned to read and write from the *missionaries* who came to teach them about Christianity. By the late 1700s Indians were using this knowledge to express their own ideas and to preserve their traditions for future generations.

Samson Occom was the first Indian writer to have a work *published* in English. Occom was a member of the Mohegan tribe of eastern Connecticut. By the time of Occom's birth in 1723, most of the Mohegans' homeland had been settled by English colonists, and the Mohegans had begun to adopt the ways and religion of the English. Occom became a missionary and spent three years in England, where he raised money for the Indian Charity School in Hanover, New Hampshire. Later that school became Dartmouth College.

Occom's most famous piece of writing was a sermon that was published in 1772. Occom wrote the sermon for the execution of Moses Paul, a Mohegan Indian who was convicted of murder. Moses Paul was drunk when he committed the murder. Occom's sermon deals with the devastating effects of alcohol on Indian lives.

During the 19th century, *autobiographies*, or life histories, written by Native Americans became very popular with non-Indian readers. These autobiographies often told of the unfair treatment that Native Americans experienced at the hands of the U.S. government. They have also helped to preserve tribal customs and history for readers in the present day.

The first Native American autobiography published was *A Son of the Forest* by William Apes, a member of the Pequot tribe. The Pequots were once the most feared tribe in New England. In 1637 the English

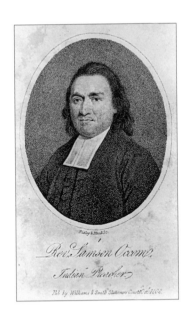

Samson Occom was the first Native American to publish a work in English.

and several local tribes waged war on the Pequots. By the end of the Pequot War, many Pequots had been killed or enslaved. The survivors eventually settled on reservations in Connecticut, where their descendants still live today.

William Apes was born in 1798. He spent most of his childhood working as a servant for white families. Apes converted to Christianity and, as an adult, became a minister. He published his autobiography in 1829. In it he expressed his anger at the white people with whom he had lived as a child. They had taught him to be afraid of other Indians, and they often threatened to punish him by sending him into the forest to live with the Indians. In his autobiography he writes:

> The great fear I entertained of my brethren, was occasioned by the many stories I had heard of their cruelty towards the whites—how they were in the habit of killing and scalping men, women and children. But the whites did not tell me that they were in a great majority of instances the aggressors—that they had imbrued their hands in the life blood of my brethren, driven them from their once peaceful and happy homes—that they introduced among them the fatal and exterminating diseases of civilized life. If the whites had told me how cruel they had been to the poor Indian, I should have apprehended as much harm from them.

William Apes was one of the most force-ful Indian writers of the early 1800s. In addi-tion to his autobiography, he wrote books that described the unfair treatment of the Indians of New England at the hands of the English and Americans.

In the 19th century, Native American authors began to use their talents to record the histories of their tribes. These histories had been passed down through the genera-tions as oral traditions. As the ancient Indian ways of life came to an end, the tribal histo-ries were in danger of disappearing forever. The authors of these accounts hoped to leave a record of their histories for future generations. They also wanted white read-ers to recognize that the tribes' long histories entitled them to the land that they occupied.

George Copway, a member of the Ojibwa tribe, wrote *Traditional History and Characteristic Sketches of the Ojibway Nation*. In this book, which was published in 1850, Copway emphasizes the importance of the oral tradition to Indian history.

Like many Native American authors, Copway combined his life history with the history of his tribe. His autobiography, *Life, History, and Travels of Kah-ge-ga-gah-bowh*, is a mixture of Ojibwa myths, history, and

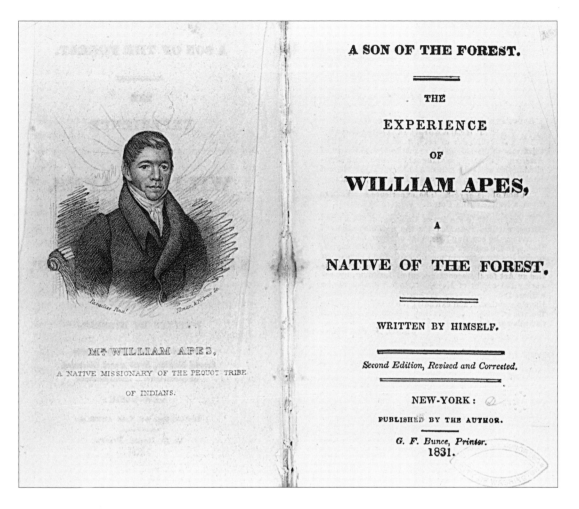

A SON OF THE FOREST.

THE

EXPERIENCE

OF

WILLIAM APES,

A

NATIVE OF THE FOREST.

WRITTEN BY HIMSELF.

Second Edition, Revised and Corrected.

NEW-YORK:

PUBLISHED BY THE AUTHOR.

G. F. Bunce, Printer.
1831.

Mr. WILLIAM APES,

A NATIVE MISSIONARY OF THE PEQUOT TRIBE

OF INDIANS.

The popularity of Native American autobiographies began with William Apes's A Son of the Forest.

Copway's own experiences. Copway tells of his early life in Canada, where he lived a traditional Ojibwa life. At the age of nine, he was converted to Christianity. He went on to marry a white woman and work as a missionary in Wisconsin, Minnesota, and Canada. Although he believed that it was important to convert Indians to Christianity, he was proud of the Ojibwas' history and valued the traditional wisdom he had learned from his father. The pictures of Indian family life in his book are warm and tender. They show a completely different image of the Indian from those depicted in books written by whites at the time. The book became popular among white readers and helped to change their opinions of the Indians.

In *Life Among the Piutes,* Sarah Winnemucca describes her tribe's customs and its struggles with whites. The Paiute Indians once controlled a vast territory in Nevada. By the late 19th century, most of their land had been taken and they were living in poverty. Winnemucca spent much of her life trying to improve relations between the Paiutes, the white settlers, and the U.S. government. But her tribe's situation grew worse in 1879, when Winnemucca and a group of Paiutes were forced to move to a reservation in Washington State. Conditions on the reservation were so poor that many people died during the harsh winter.

Winnemucca began giving lectures to white audiences to gain support for the Paiutes' rights. During her lifetime she would give more than 300 speeches. She reached even more people with her book, which came out in 1883. In the following passage from *Life Among the Piutes*, Winnemucca *criticizes* white people for their prejudice against the Indians. She points out that many of the Christian values that whites tried to teach the Indians were already an important part of Paiute society:

> But the whites have not waited to find out how good the Indians were, and what ideas they had of God, just like those of Jesus, who called him Father, just as my people do, and told men to do to others as they would be done by, just as my people teach their children to do. My people teach their children never to make fun of any one, no matter how they look. . . . If you make fun of bad persons, you make yourself beneath them. Be kind to all, both poor and rich, and feed all that come to your wigwam, and your name can be spoken of by every one far and near. In this way you will make many friends for yourself. Be kind both to bad and good, for you don't know your own heart. This is the way my people teach their children. It was handed down from father to son for many generations. I never in my life saw our children rude as I have seen white children and grown people in the streets.

While many Native American authors were writing about their own experiences and the histories of their tribes, John Rollin Ridge was one of the few Indians in the 1800s who wrote fiction (stories that are not based on real events). Ridge, who was born in 1827, was half-Cherokee. His grandfather had been one of the Cherokees' most powerful leaders before the tribe was forced to leave its homeland in the southeastern United States and move to a reservation in Oklahoma.

Ridge wrote under the name Yellow Bird, the English translation of his Cherokee name, Cheesquatalawny. He wrote for newspapers in San Francisco and eventually became the owner and editor of several newspapers in California.

In 1854, Ridge's book *The Life and Adventures of Joaquín Murieta* was the first novel to be published by an Indian. It tells the story of a hardworking man who is part Indian and part Spanish. Much like the Cherokees were, Joaquín is driven from his land by greedy white men. After his brother is murdered, Joaquín seeks revenge. The book then follows his actions as Joaquín becomes a fearless leader of his people:

> He dashed along that fearful trail as he had been mounted upon a spirit-steed, shouting as he passed:
> "I am Joaquín! Kill me if you can!"
> Shot after shot came clanging around his head, and bullet after bullet flattened on the wall of salt at his right. In the midst of the first firing, his hat was knocked from his head, and left his long black hair streaming behind him.

Joaquín Murieta and his Robin Hood-like adventures became very popular and *inspired* many Mexican-American writers.

At the end of the 19th century, the poetry of Emily Pauline Johnson gained much attention in Canada, the United States, and England. Johnson, the daughter of a Mohawk chief and an English woman, was born on the Six Nations Reserve in Ontario, Canada. (The Mohawks were one of the six nations of the Iroquois Confederacy.)

Johnson published three books of poetry between 1895 and 1912: *White Wampum, Canadian Born,* and *Flint and Feather.* She was also one of the first Native American women to have stories published. *The Moccasin Maker,* a collection of her short stories, came out in 1913. Most of her stories are about Indian and non-Indian women in Canada. Many describe the love that Indian mothers feel for their children. Other stories focus on the great strength of the pioneer women who made homes for their families in new and unfamiliar places.

In some of her stories, Johnson writes about the problems of *mixed-blood* women—women who are part Indian and part white. The mixed-blood's search to fit in later became a major theme in Native American *literature*. Johnson's most popular

An 1859 drawing of the hero of John Rollin Ridge's The Life and Adventures of Joaquín Murieta.

story with this theme is "A Red Girl's Reasoning." In this story a mixed-blood woman decides that she must remain true to her Indian values even though her decision means she must leave the white husband she loves.

Emily Pauline Johnson and the other early Native American writers helped to establish a written Indian tradition. Many authors in the 20th century have read these early writers and have learned from them. They have also found the inspiration to write about their own histories and to create their own poems, stories, and novels. ▲

CHAPTER 4

Indian Writers 1900–1967

By 1900, most Native Americans had been forced to give up their traditional ways. The U.S. government had relocated many tribes to Indian Territory, the present-day state of Oklahoma. The loss of their homelands caused the Indians terrible hardship. Thousands of Native Americans starved during the move to reservations. Others, weakened by harsh conditions, died of disease. Those who survived the forced move often found that their new land was impossible to farm or that there were no animals to hunt.

Whites who were disturbed by this massive suffering believed that the Indians' only hope was to abandon their traditions and to learn to live like white Americans. Boarding schools were established to educate Indian children. By removing children from their families, educators hoped to raise generations of Native Americans who would not know their tribes' languages and traditions. Many of the Native American authors who wrote in the early 20th century attended these schools, and some even wrote about their school experiences.

Charles Eastman, one of the most popular Indian writers of the early 1900s, was greatly affected by the forces that changed the Indians' lives. Eastman, a Santee Sioux originally named Ohiyesa, was born in 1858 near Redwood Falls, Minnesota. As a young boy, Ohiyesa led the traditional life of a Santee Sioux. But he lived to see that way of life disappear.

When Ohiyesa was 15 years old, his life changed dramatically. His father, Many Lightnings, who had been imprisoned after taking part in a Sioux rebellion, returned home. While in prison, Many Lightnings had accepted Christianity and learned to live like a white man. He wanted his son to do the same. Ohiyesa was baptized and sent to

Indian schools such as this one, on the Pine Ridge Reservation in South Dakota, were intended to separate Native American children from their families and to teach them to live like white Americans.

boarding school. Ohiyesa became Charles Alexander Eastman.

Eastman *adapted* well to his new life. He excelled in school and went on to attend Dartmouth College. In 1890 he completed medical school at Boston University and moved to the Pine Ridge Reservation in South Dakota. He was the only doctor in the area on December 29, 1890, when a battle broke out between the U.S. Army and the Sioux. More than 300 Sioux (mostly women and children) were killed in this fight, which came to be known as the Battle of Wounded Knee. Eastman worked through the night tending to the wounded in a crowded chapel. Later Eastman described the event:

"We tore out the pews and covered the floor with hay and quilts. There we laid the poor creatures side by side in rows, and the night was devoted to caring for them as best we could. The suffering was terrible."

On the reservation Eastman met and married Elaine Goodale, a teacher from Massachusetts. With the help of his new wife, Eastman began to write about his life as a Sioux. He hoped to save at least the memory of his tribe's traditions.

Eastman's first autobiographical book, *Indian Boyhood*, was published in 1902 and became a best-seller. In it he describes the life he had led before he went away to school. He tried to help his non-Indian readers to appreciate the Sioux way of life: "What boy would not be an Indian for a while when he thinks of the freest life in the world? This life was mine. Everyday there was a real hunt. There was real game."

In his second autobiographical book, *From the Deep Woods to Civilization*, Eastman tells of his experiences as an adult. He criticizes the U.S. government for its treatment of the Sioux, and especially for the hunger and poverty of those living on reservations.

In all of his writings, Eastman revealed to white readers the values, customs, litera-

Charles Eastman wrote about the joy and freedom of growing up in Santee Sioux society.

ture, and history of the Sioux. In *Red Hunters and the Animal People,* Eastman tells animal and adventure stories he learned as a boy. *Old Indian Days* also draws on Native American tradition while focusing on stories about warriors and women. *Wigwam Evenings: Sioux Folktales Retold* is a book of stories for children.

Eastman also worked for the Boy Scouts of America, leading scout troops through the woods and teaching the children about the outdoors. He wrote a book called *Indian Scout Tales* for the Boy Scouts and Campfire Girls. The following year, the Eastmans opened the School of the Woods, a summer camp in New Hampshire. Campers learned Native American dances, archery, and other traditional skills.

Eastman's books inspired other Sioux writers to record their lives. Luther Standing Bear attended the Carlisle Indian School, which was founded in 1879 to educate young Indians. He later joined Buffalo Bill's Wild West Show and then moved to California where he became an actor, lecturer, and volunteer for Indian causes. Standing Bear's *My People, the Sioux* was published in 1928. In it he describes his journey to Carlisle, Pennsylvania, and his life at the school there. In 1931, he published *My Indian Boyhood,* a book for young readers. In his last book, *Land of the Spotted Eagle,* Standing Bear describes Sioux beliefs and customs and criticizes white people's treatment of Indians.

In 1900 and 1901, the essays of Zitkala-Sa (a Yankton Sioux also known as Gertrude Bonnin) were published in popular magazines and were later assembled into a book called *American Indian Stories.* Zitkala-Sa was born in 1876 on the Yankton reservation in South Dakota. In one essay, she describes the freedom and happiness of her childhood: "I was a wild little girl of seven. Loosely clad in a slip of brown buckskin, and light-footed with a pair of soft moccasins on my feet, I was as free as the wind that blew my hair, and no less spirited than a bounding deer. These were my mother's pride,—my wild freedom and overflowing spirits."

This life came to an end when Zitkala-Sa was eight years old. She was sent to a school in Indiana, where she suddenly lost her freedom and had to adjust to rigid rules. Zitkala-Sa recalled her first day at the school, when all the Indian children had their long hair cut:

> I cried aloud, shaking my head all the while until I felt the cold blade of the scissors against

Evening in the Lodge, *an illustration from Charles Eastman's* Indian Boyhood.

my neck, and heard them gnaw off one of my thick braids. Then I lost my spirit. Since the day I was taken from my mother I had suffered extreme indignities. People had stared at me. I had been tossed about in the air like a wooden puppet. And now my long hair was shingled like a coward's! In my anguish I groaned for my mother, but no one came to comfort me. Not a soul reasoned quietly with me, as my own mother used to do; for now I was only one of many little animals driven by a herder.

Although adjusting to life at school was difficult, when Zitkala-Sa returned home three years later she found that she no longer fit in. Now she was caught between two worlds and felt that she did not belong in either. This feeling stayed with her throughout her life. She continued her education but would not give up her Indian ways.

Zitkala-Sa used her education to help her fellow Native Americans. In her book *Old Indian Legends* she helped preserve the traditions of the Yankton Sioux by recording the stories that she had learned from the elders of the tribe. She was a member of the Society of American Indians, a group of well-educated Native Americans that lobbied for the right of tribes to govern themselves. And in 1926 she formed the National Council of American Indians.

Francis La Flesche was another author who wrote about his life experiences. La Flesche was born in 1857 into the Omaha tribe of Nebraska. He became one of the first Indian *anthropologists*, and he wrote books recording the traditions of his people and explaining their culture to outsiders.

One of his books, *The Middle Five* (1900), contains his memories of the school he attended on his reservation. Students lived at the school, going home to their villages only on Saturdays. He describes his best friend, Brush; their teacher, whom all the boys called Gray-beard; the strict discipline of the school; and the fun the children had playing outdoors and telling stories at night in the dormitory. *The Middle Five* is a lively and often amusing description of what it was like to be an Omaha child in the mid-19th century.

As an adult, La Flesche worked for the U.S. government in the Bureau of Indian Affairs, and later at the Bureau of American Ethnology. Though he earned a law degree and became a respected scholar in the English-speaking world, he equally valued his tribal education. He wanted his writing to teach white people about the dignity and sophistication of his own culture.

Will Rogers was the most famous Native American writer of the 1920s. Rogers was born in 1879 into a prominent Cherokee family in Indian Territory. When he was 18, he left school against his father's wishes and became a cowboy.

Rogers traveled around the world, and in South Africa he joined a Wild West show. Wild West shows were very popular in the United States and were spreading to other countries. They featured sharpshooting, roping, trick riding, and pretend fights between men dressed as cowboys and Indians.

By 1915, Rogers was a popular performer in the United States. He joined the *Ziegfeld Follies*, a New York stage show, in which he continued to do roping tricks and started to talk in his act as well. Soon Rogers became famous for his jokes and comments about the news of the day. These ideas were collected in two books, *Roger-isms: The Cowboy Philosopher on the Peace Conference* and *Roger-isms: The Cowboy Philosopher on Prohibition*, both of which were published in 1919.

During this same period Rogers began to act in movies. In 1918, he played the part of a tramp in the film *Laughing Bill*

Hyde. Audiences loved him, and he went on to act in about 30 other movies. In the early 1930s, he was one of Hollywood's biggest stars. In many of his films, Rogers plays the part of the trickster, like the traditional Coyote character in Indian myths.

In 1922, Rogers was hired to write a column for the *New York Times.* In his articles, Rogers liked to make fun of politicians and prominent businessmen. The column was printed in many newspapers all over the country.

The *Saturday Evening Post* sent Rogers to Europe in 1926 to write a series of columns. While abroad Rogers sent a telegram to his editor at the *New York Times*, who thought it was so funny that he not only printed it in the newspaper, but he asked Rogers to keep writing to him. Eventually Rogers's telegrams appeared every day in more than 500 American newspapers.

During the height of the Great Depression, Rogers, who was now one of the most popular entertainers in the country, traveled to 50 different cities to raise money for the Red Cross so that it could continue to feed the nation's hungry. Rogers insisted that part of the money he raised go to the people of the

continued on page 57

Writer and performer Will Rogers was one of the most beloved entertainers in America during the early 20th century.

PAINTING TRADITION

For centuries, Native Americans have used not only oral and written literatures but also painting to express their views of themselves and the world around them.

Indian painting has changed over time. Before the 19th century, Native Americans used colors made from vegetables and minerals and painted in traditional styles. But they gradually abandoned these homemade pigments for manufactured watercolors and oils because the newer paints were brighter and easier to use. At the same time, some Indian artists began drawing in the style of white Americans and Europeans, so that they could sell their work to non-Indians.

Even so, many of today's Native American painters choose to honor their past through their artwork. Some imitate the clear lines and flat colors found in traditional Indian hide paintings and pottery decoration. Others celebrate their heritage through the content of their art, depicting ancient Indian stories that tell how the world began or adventure stories about tribal heroes. These painters use their art to tell old stories in a new way to a new audience.

A detail from The Legend of the Snake Clan, *a hide painting by 20th-century Hopi artist Fred Kabotie.*

The Iroquois story of creation is depicted in this 1980 painting entitled **Creations Battle** *by Mohawk artist John Fadden. The conflict between good and evil in the universe is represented by the struggle between Sky Woman's sons, The Good Twin and The Evil Twin. The Good Twin created all the good in the universe, including plants, animals, rivers, and streams. To counteract his brother's work, The Evil Twin produced poisonous plants, thorns, diseases, and monsters. However, The Evil Twin was not ultimately powerful enough to triumph in the creation battle. As a final stroke, The Good Twin created human beings to enjoy all the good he had made for them.*

A Navajo creation myth is represented in the 1938 painting Sun King and His Wife by Gerald Nailor. Pictured is the Sun's visit with Changing Woman, who as a result gives birth to twin sons, Child Born of Water and Monster Slayer. During the twins' childhood, Changing Woman creates the Navajo people from a mixture of cornmeal and scrapings of her own skin.

Navajo artist Andy Tsinajinnie portrays his tribe's origin story in The Fourth World (1960). In the center of this painting are the three lower worlds through which the Navajo believe all creatures of the universe had to travel before they could reach the world they now inhabit. In each world, humans co-exist peacefully with other animals. Thus, the story illustrates the importance of maintaining harmony within a group, a value the Navajo cherish.

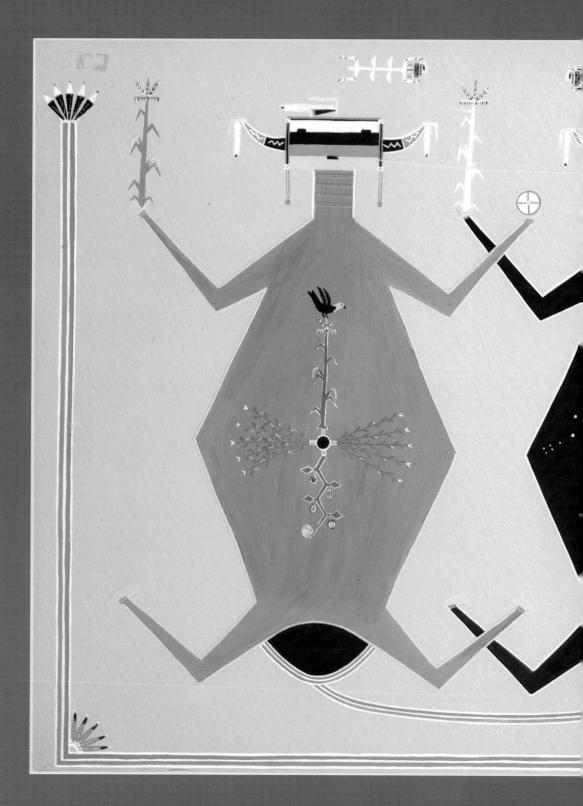

The divine creators of the first human couple are illustrated in **Mother Earth and Father Sky, Male Shootingway,** *a 1936 watercolor copy of a Navajo sand painting. According to Navajo and Pueblo narratives, the pair are the ancestors of the Hero Twins, who vanquished the forces of evil in order to make the world safe for humans to inhabit.*

Mother Earth is colored turquoise and holds a corn plant and a basket containing corn pollen. In the center of her body is the water that covered the earth when people had first journeyed from the underworld to the earth's surface. From the water's surface sprout four sacred plants brought up from below—corn, beans, squash, and tobacco.

Father Sky's body is black and covered with white markings representing the Milky Way, crescent moon, and constellations. He holds an ear of corn and a blue basket with corn pollen sprinkled in four directions.

The figures of Father Sky and Mother Earth have identical shapes, symbolizing cosmic harmony. They are also linked by the lines of sacred pollen between their mouths and between their reproductive organs. Both are wearing buffalo horns marked with lightning and identical headdresses of turkey and eagle feathers.

The character of Coyote appears in many tribes' traditional stories. Coyote is usually a clever trickster but is often outsmarted by the victims of his pranks. The traditional figure of the Coyote trickster has been revitalized through the work of Maidu artist Harry Fonseca. In his series of Coyote paintings, Fonseca blends old beliefs and stories with elements of modern art. Fonseca says, "I believe my Coyote paintings to be the most contemporary statement I have painted in regard to traditional belief and contemporary reality. I have taken a universal Indian image, Coyote, and have placed him in a contemporary setting." Fonseca has captured Coyote in many identities, painting the trickster as an actor, a rock star, and a tourist. This work, Koshare with Watermelon (1983), depicts two coyotes as Pueblo clowns.

Eskimo Hunter (1959) by Kivetoruk Moses portrays the story of an Inuit hunter who is captured by a huge eagle. Attempting to escape, the Inuit wounds the eagle's leg with a knife. Listening to the heartbeat of the dying eagle, the hunter learns the rhythm that the Inuit play on the drum to accompany their ceremonial dancing.

Saynday, a supernatural being who created the Kiowa people, is portrayed in Sharron Ahtone Harjo's 1972 work, Saynday and the Prairie Dogs. *In the story depicted, Saynday has tricked a group of prairie dogs into closing their eyes and then kills them one by one. He spares the one animal who is smart enough to keep her eyes open and chooses her to become the mother of all prairie dogs.*

Hopi artist Fred Kabotie's hide painting, **The Legend of the Snake Clan**, depicts the story of Tiyo, the son of a village chief. Tiyo encounters a kiva (religious house) whose members are able to turn themselves into snakes by putting on snakeskin costumes. With the help of Spider Woman (a figure in Navajo mythology), Tiyo is able to overpower the snake people and is accepted into the clan. Tiyo marries one of the Snake Clan women. Their children become the founders of the Snake Clan at the village of Walpi.

continued from page 48

Cherokee tribe.

Will Rogers's intelligence, honesty, and generosity were so admired that he was asked to run for president, but he refused. Rogers's career was cut short in 1935, when he was killed in a plane crash in Alaska. More than 50,000 people attended his funeral.

In addition to Will Rogers's humor, the 1920s saw the publication of the first novel by a Native American woman. Mourning Dove's *Co-ge-we-a, the Half-Blood* appeared in 1927. Like Emily Pauline Johnson, who wrote almost 15 years earlier, Mourning Dove (a Salish Indian from Washington State) wrote about the life of a mixed-blood woman. In one episode, Co-ge-we-a, dressed as a white woman, enters a "ladies' " horse race. The judge will not let her have the prize she has won, however, because she is a "squaw." When she then enters a race for Indian women, she is told that the race is for "Indians and not for breeds!" Neither whites nor Indians entirely accept her.

Coyote Stories is a collection of stories that Mourning Dove heard from her relatives and the older members of her tribe. Mourning Dove also began writing her auto- biography. Although she died before it was completed, her writings were edited and published as *Mourning Dove: A Salish Autobiography.* In this book, Mourning Dove describes her own life and the role of women in Indian society.

During the 1920s, John Milton Oskison published more work than any other Indian writer working during that decade. Oskison was one-eighth Cherokee and was raised in Indian Territory. After graduating from Stanford University, he went on to become an editor and writer for *Collier's,* a popular magazine of the time. His articles on Indian affairs also appeared in other magazines and in newspapers. He published three novels, *Wild Harvest, Black Jack Davy,* and *Brothers Three.* He also wrote *Tecumseh and His Times,* a *biography* of the Shawnee leader.

In the first half of the 20th century, anthropologists and others interested in Native American customs began to collect Indian life stories. *Black Elk Speaks,* published in 1932, is one of the most popular books of this type. Black Elk was a Teton Sioux holy man. Born in 1863, he lived through the most turbulent time in the history of his tribe. At the age of 13, he took part in the Battle of the Little Bighorn—where the Sioux defeated U.S. troops led by General Custer.

He also witnessed the massacre at Wounded Knee in 1890, where U.S. soldiers killed over 300 Sioux.

In 1930 Black Elk was interviewed by the poet John G. Neihardt, who was conducting research for a poem about the American West. But Black Elk wanted Neihardt to write about the religion of the Sioux so that the knowledge he had gained from his ancestors would not be lost. The two men talked for two weeks, and the result was *Black Elk Speaks.* The book tells the story of Black Elk's life and his experiences with his religion. It also describes the values and beliefs of the Sioux and their customs both before and after they were forced to move to reservations.

During the 1920s and 1930s, more and more Native American writers went to college. As a result, their work grew more sophisticated. Two of the best writers of this period were D'Arcy McNickle and John Joseph Mathews. Both of these writers focused on the importance of keeping traditional tribal ways.

John Joseph Mathews's first book, *Wah' Kon-Tah,* was published in 1932. It was based on the journal of the first U.S. government agent to work among the Osages, and it portrays the Osages' determination to

Osage historian and novelist John Joseph Mathews in his home in Osage County, Oklahoma.

hold on to their tribal ways despite the agent's attempts to lead them down the white man's road. In later years, Mathews wrote *The Osages: Children of the Middle Waters*, a history of his tribe.

Mathews wrote one novel, *Sundown*. It tells the story of Challenge Windzer, who is torn between the beliefs of his Osage mother, who wants to preserve tribal traditions, and his mixed-blood father, who wants to fit into white society. Windzer rejects the ways of the Osages but does not feel at home in modern America. Unable to cope in either the Osage or the non-Indian world, Windzer becomes an alcoholic.

D'Arcy McNickle was a mixed-blood of Cree ancestry on his mother's side and white ancestry on his father's side. When he was a child, his family was adopted into the Flathead tribe. McNickle attended the University of Montana, Oxford University in England, and Grenoble University in France. Back in the United States, he worked for the Bureau of Indian Affairs, the government agency responsible for Native Americans. Later McNickle helped to found the National Congress of American Indians.

In 1936, McNickle published an outstanding novel, *The Surrounded*, in which he describes the breakdown of tribal religion and values as tribes lose their land to whites. However, the novel offers hope for the survival of Native American traditions when the main character returns to the tribal culture that he had rejected.

McNickle's next novel, *The Runner in the Sun*, was written for middle school readers. McNickle tells of the adventures of Salt, a Native American boy of the Southwest who journeys to Mexico to find a way of saving his people from starvation. This novel gives many details of the ancient way of life of the Native Americans known as cliff dwellers. McNickle wrote another novel *(Wind from an Enemy)*, four histories, and a biography of the Native American writer Oliver La Farge.

Lynn Riggs was a successful playwright of the early 20th century. In 1927, his play *Big Lake* was produced on Broadway in New York City. Riggs wrote several plays set in his native Oklahoma, but only one of his plays touched on his Native American background. In *Cherokee Night* he describes the problems of mixed-bloods who have grown away from their Cherokee heritage. Riggs's 1931 play, *Green Grow the Lilacs*, was adapted into the hit musical *Oklahoma!*

Ella C. Deloria was a Sioux who grew up on the Standing Rock Indian Reservation in North and South Dakota. Deloria worked with Franz Boas, a well-known anthropologist. With Boas's encouragement Deloria wrote about the Sioux language and translated Sioux written works. In her book *Speaking of Indians*, she describes the ways in which the Sioux held on to their traditional values after moving to reservations.

Deloria also wrote a novel titled *Waterlily*. It traces the life of a Sioux woman and describes the rituals and traditions of 19th-century Sioux life. Deloria paints a touching picture of the way Sioux children were raised. In the following passage, a Sioux character expresses horror at the way white people treated their children:

> Listen! those people actually detest their children! You should see them—slapping their little ones' faces and lashing their poor little buttocks to make them cry! Why, almost any time of day if you walk near the stockade you can hear the soldiers' wives screaming at their children. Yes, they thoroughly scold them. I have never seen children treated so. . . . Only if a woman is crazy might she turn on her own child, not knowing what she did.

In the first half of the 20th century, Native Americans endured many hardships and fought continually to maintain their culture. Native American writers played an important role in saving the cultures of the tribes through both their political *activism* and their written work. Their books, articles, poems, and plays serve as a reminder of the strength and values of Native American cultures. They inform writers of today and inspire writers of the future. ▲

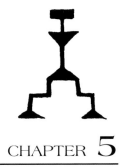

CHAPTER 5

Literary Explosion: 1968 to the Present

The 1960s were a time of great changes in the United States. Minorities fought for their rights and overturned laws that discriminated against them. Native Americans took part in this struggle, and as a result they began to take more and more pride in their heritage. This pride inspired a surge in Native American literature.

In 1969, N. Scott Momaday won a Pulitzer Prize (one of the most important awards for American literature) for his novel *House Made of Dawn*. Momaday, a member of the Kiowa tribe, was born in 1934 in Lawton, Oklahoma. He spent much of his childhood in the southwestern United States on the

Navajo, San Carlos Apache, and Jemez Pueblo reservations. Momaday holds a Ph.D. in English and is a professor at the University of Arizona.

In *House Made of Dawn*, Momaday focuses on the problems of modern-day Native Americans. He writes about the importance of the oral tradition and of rituals and ceremonies. The book was widely praised, more so than any Native American novel had been before.

In 1969, Momaday published *Way to Rainy Mountain*. In this book he tells of the Kiowas' origins and their relocation to Oklahoma. He describes their life both before and after the reservation period, as well as his own search for his tribal roots. He also includes Kiowa myths and history.

Leslie Marmon Silko is another author who has written about the importance of tradition to modern-day Native Americans. Silko is of Pueblo, Mexican, and white ancestry. She was raised in Laguna Pueblo, New Mexico, and she graduated from the University of New Mexico. In 1977 she published *Ceremony*. The main character in the novel is a Pueblo who is a veteran of World War II. After suffering from a mental breakdown, he is healed by traditional Laguna stories and rituals. Silko has also written short stories and poems. Many of her stories are modern versions of traditional myths including such ancient characters as Coyote, the trickster.

Another Native American writer who became popular in the 1970s is James Welch, who comes from a Blackfoot and Gros Ventre background. In his first two novels, *Winter in the Blood* and *The Death of Jim Loney*, the main character searches his family's past to try to gain some understanding of the present. In *Fools Crow*, Welch tells the story of a Blackfoot warrior and medicine man during the 1870s, when white settlers were taking over his Montana homeland. Welch gives a colorful description of traditional Blackfoot life, including oral traditions and ceremonies.

Gerald Vizenor, an Ojibwa Indian, is a professor at the University of California at Berkeley. Among his many books are *Wordarrows, Earthdivers*, and *The People Named the Chippewa*. Each of these deals with the hardships of Native Americans who have to adjust to the ways of white Americans. He includes the true stories of people who have suffered through this experience. One example from *Earthdivers* is the story of Dane Michael White, a 13-year-old Sioux runaway who hanged

Louise Erdrich and Michael Dorris are popular modern writers who draw inspiration from their Native American heritage.

himself in a Minnesota jail while waiting to hear if he would be sent to a foster home or allowed to live with his grandmother.

Louise Erdrich is another popular Ojibwa novelist. Erdrich was born in North Dakota and attended Dartmouth College and The Johns Hopkins University. Her novels

Love Medicine, The Beet Queen, Tracks, and *The Bingo Palace* explore the complicated relationships between Native Americans, their families, mixed-bloods, and whites. Erdrich has also published two books of poetry, edited a collection of short stories, and written a book about her experiences as a writer and a mother.

Louise Erdrich and her husband, Michael Dorris, cowrote *The Crown of Columbus*. This novel tells the story of Vivian Two Star—a mixed-blood Native American and professor of Native American studies. While writing an article on Christopher Columbus, Vivian discovers part of his long-lost diary. The mysteries of the diary lead her to an adventure in the Bahamas in search of further clues about Columbus's voyages.

In addition to working with Louise Erdrich, Michael Dorris has written many of his own books. A member of the Modoc tribe, he grew up in Kentucky, Washington, Idaho, and Montana. Dorris attended Georgetown University and Yale University. For several years he was a professor of Native American studies at Dartmouth College. He is now a full-time writer.

In 1989, Dorris published his first novel, *A Yellow Raft on Blue Water*. The book is set on a reservation in Montana and tells the story of three generations of women, including a 15-year-old girl whose mother is Native American and whose father is African American.

Dorris has also written two books for young readers. *Morning Girl* is narrated (or told) by 12-year-old Morning Girl and her younger brother, Star Boy. They are Taino Indians living in the Bahamas in the 1400s. Morning Girl and Star Boy describe the life of their tribe as it was before Columbus landed on their island in 1492. In the last chapter, Columbus describes the people that he finds on the island. After getting to know the Taino through the eyes of Morning Girl and Star Boy, the reader sees just how little Columbus understood about the tribe.

Guests, Dorris's second book for young readers, was published in 1994. It is the story of the first Thanksgiving, told from the viewpoint of a Native American boy named Moss. Moss is impatient to grow up, yet he is afraid of change. His father has invited strangers to share the tribe's harvest meal, but Moss does not want to feed the guests with their "odd clothes and strange hair." He runs into the woods instead of helping with the preparations. While he is away, he learns something about himself.

Louise Erdrich and Michael Dorris both

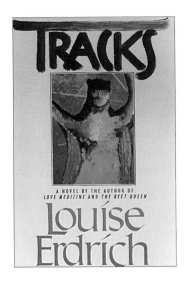

Louise Erdrich's Tracks *was a best-seller in 1988.*

have published best-selling books and have received National Book Critics Circle awards.

Another well-known writer of books for young people is Jamake Highwater, an author of Blackfoot and Cherokee heritage. In 1978 he received one of the most important awards given to authors of children's books when his novel *Anpao: An American Indian Odyssey* was named a Newbery Honor Book. This book tells the story of Anpao, a young man who must journey to the home of the Sun and ask for permission to marry the beautiful Ko-ko-mik-e-is. The adventures of Anpao and the characters he encounters along the way are based on the oral traditions of the Indians of the Great Plains and the Southwest.

Highwater also wrote a series of novels that trace the life of Amana, a member of the Blood tribe of the Northern Plains. In *Legend Days*, Amana sees her tribe's way of life coming to an end as white settlers move into her homeland. At the age of 11, Amana is orphaned during an outbreak of smallpox, a disease that came from Europe and killed huge numbers of Native Americans. She runs away from her people to avoid catching the disease. After wandering alone in the wilderness she is taken in and protected by grandfather fox, who gives her a valuable gift: the bravery and skill of a hunter and warrior. But she may only use her gift when, in time of need, she hears the song of the foxes in her heart. When she returns to her people she must learn the skills and responsibilities of the women in her tribe. At first this frustrates her, as she wants to go off on the hunt instead of working in the camp with the women. But she eventually grows to appreciate her female traits and to unite them with the warrior inside her.

In *The Ceremony of Innocence*, Amana has a daughter named Jamika, who grows up without her tribe's ancient traditions. Amana worries that the history and wisdom she inherited from her elders is going to disappear with the younger generation. But she gains hope from her grandson Sitko, who loves learning the old stories and ceremonies. *I Wear the Morning Star* focuses on Sitko's experiences in a boarding school and the ways in which he keeps his heritage alive.

Another of Jamake Highwater's novels, *Eyes of Darkness*, is based on the life of Charles Eastman.

Joseph Bruchac, who is of Abenaki and European heritage, has written a number of books for young readers. Bruchac's poems and stories have been included in more than 500 books and magazines. He has written novels, picture books, and poetry and has retold many traditional stories. In 1992, Bruchac organized the first North American Native Writers Festival in Norman, Oklahoma.

Bruchac has written collections of traditional stories for young readers, including *Iroquois Stories*, *Turtle Meat and Other Stories*, and *Return of the Sun: Native American Tales of the Northwest Woodlands*. His award-winning *Thirteen Moons on a Turtle's Back* celebrates the seasons of the year in poems, which are based on Native American legends. Bruchac's picture books include *The First Strawberries* (a Cherokee tale of how strawberries were created) and *The Great Ball Game* (a Muskogee story of a game between birds and other animals). In 1993, Bruchac published *Dawn Land*, a novel that is set 10,000 years ago among the Abenakis and other Northeastern tribes.

Bruchac coauthored *Keepers of the Earth*, *Keepers of the Animals*, and *Keepers of Life*. These books contain Native American stories and activities that make readers aware of people's responsibility to protect the environment.

Martin Cruz Smith is the author of such thrillers as Gorky Park, *which was made into a popular movie.*

In addition to being a popular writer, Bruchac is a professional storyteller. He has made recordings of ancient stories so that they can be enjoyed the way they were intended to be: by listening. Storytelling, he says, helps to keep us connected with the people of the past.

Martin Cruz Smith is a popular mystery writer who is of Senecu del Sur and Yaqui heritage. His *Nightwing* and *Stallion Gate* both feature Native American characters who fight in wars overseas and return home feeling separated from their people and traditions. Smith's 1981 thriller, *Gorky Park*, is set in Russia and was made into a successful film. Smith has also written a sequel called *Polar Star*.

Simon Ortiz is a well-known Acoma Pueblo poet. He has also written three picture books for young readers: *The People Shall Continue, The Importance of Childhood,* and *Blue and Red.* Ortiz has used his knowledge of traditional stories in his poems. In "Telling About Coyote" he describes how Coyote lost his fur coat in a card game.

Other Native American poets include Linda Allen, Ray Young Bear, and Joy Harjo. Harjo has published three books of poetry: *In Mad Love and War, She Had Some*

Joy Harjo is one of the many talented female poets who keep the Native American literary tradition alive.

Horses, and *What Moon Drove Me to This*.

The people mentioned in this book are only a few of the many Native American authors who have kept alive the traditions of their ancestors. Their works help us to understand the history, the beliefs, and the wisdom of the civilizations that once peopled this land. ▲

GLOSSARY

activism	speaking out and taking action to bring about change
adapt	to learn to survive in a new environment
anthropologist	a person who studies the cultures of groups of people
autobiography	a book in which the author tells his or her life story
biography	a history of a person's life
chant	a song that is sung in a steady, unchanging rhythm
criticize	to point out the mistakes or bad behavior of a person or group
culture	the traditions, religious beliefs, language, art, and way of life of a people
eloquently	in a beautiful and convincing manner
inspire	to influence a person in a way that leads him or her to think or act differently
literature	written stories and histories; oral literature is remembered and spoken aloud but not written down
missionaries	people who teach Christianity in non-Christian communities
mixed-blood	a person who has both Indian and non-Indian ancestors
myth	a traditional story that explains the beliefs of a people and their understanding of the world
novel	a book that describes imaginary events
oral tradition	stories, songs, and ceremonies that are told through many generations
publish	to print the work of an author and make it available to readers
reservation	an area of land set aside by the U.S. government for use by Native Americans
values	ideas that guide people's behavior

CHRONOLOGY

1772 Mohegan Samson Occom publishes *Sermon Preached at the Execution of Moses Paul, an Indian*—the first work published in English by a Native American

1829 William Apes, a Pequot, publishes *A Son of the Forest*, the first autobiography by a Native American

1850 *Traditional History and Characteristic Sketches of the Ojibway Nation* by Ojibwa George Copway appears

1854 Cherokee John Rollin Ridge, or Yellow Bird, publishes the first novel by a Native American, *The Life and Times of Don Joaquin Murieta*

1883 The first book by a Native American woman is published: Sarah Winnemucca's *Life Among the Piutes*

1902 Charles Eastman's *Indian Boyhood*, an autobiographical work about growing up a Santee Sioux, appears

1919 Cherokee Will Rogers, a cowboy-turned-Broadway-performer and the most famous Native American writer of the 1920s, publishes his *Roger-isms: The Cowboy Philosopher on the Peace Conference and Roger-isms: The Cowboy Philosopher on Prohibition*

1927 Mourning Dove, a Salish, publishes the first novel by a Native American woman, *Co-ge-we-a, The Half-Blood*

1931 Lynn Riggs, a playwright of Cherokee ancestry, publishes *Green Grow the Lilacs*, later adapted to become the hit musical *Oklahoma!*

1932 *Black Elk Speaks*, the popular life story of a Teton Sioux holy man, appears

1936 D'Arcy McNickle, a mixed-blood of Cree ancestry, publishes *The Surrounded*, a novel describing the breakdown of religions and values as tribes lose their lands

1969 N. Scott Momaday of the Kiowa tribe wins a Pulitzer Prize for his novel *House Made of Dawn*

INDEX

ABOUT THE AUTHOR

Katherine Gleason, a freelance writer and editor, holds an M.A. from Yale University. She has worked for public television and has written for many periodicals, including the *Boston Globe, Connoisseur,* and *Lingua Franca.*